LET'S EAT!

Blue Bamboo Recipes for Gatherings

by Dennis Chan

LET'S EAT!

Blue Bamboo Recipes for Gatherings

by Dennis Chan

Blue Bamboo Publishing Co.

First Edition

Text copyright © 2022 by Dennis Chan

Photographs copyright © 2022 by Dennis Chan

All rights reserved. No part of this book may be reproduced by any means whatsoever without written permission from the publisher.

Published by Blue Bamboo Publishing Co.
10110 San Jose Boulevard
Jacksonville, Florida 32257

904.646.1478 orders
www.bluebamboojacksonville.com

Printed and designed by ABC Book Publishers, Inc.
Printed and bound in the United States of America

Text edited by Kim Benton
Photography by Dennis Chan
Book design by Jeanine Colombi-Quinn

Print ISBN # 979-8-9868305-0-6
Ebook ISBN # 979-8-9868305-1-3

Acknowledgements

I would like to first thank my parents Ming and Phyllis for all of the opportunities that you have given me. After all of these years, I am still doing just what I love.

I will be forever indebted to my mentor, Ming Tsai, for taking the chance on a culinary student and hiring me as his first intern at Blue Ginger, and for opening his restaurant up to me. He will always be referred to as the ultimate Lao Ban in my eyes.

Thanks to my cousin May, who taught me almost everything I know about the restaurant business, and hard work. Many years later, and we are still growing our business!

I must thank the staff of Blue Bamboo. The restaurant is lucky to have the staff that we do. Your hard work and care for our guests continues to wow me.

To Kim Benton, who always keeps us on schedule, whose publishing expertise made all of this happen.

Thanks to Tina York, our General Manager and lifetime friend, who makes sure that our business thrives.

Thanks to the guests of my restaurant, Blue Bamboo. Your support has been never-ending, and helped us grow our business into what we are today. We've gotten to share your lives and watch your kids grow up. Thanks for being our extended family.

And to Elizabeth, my wife, for your patience all of these years!

Celebrate the joy of friends and family with award-winning Chef Dennis Chan and the new mini cookbook "Let's Eat!" or "吃飯!," Blue Bamboo Recipes for Gatherings. Delicious Cantonese-inspired meals can be created with traditional tastes of home for any occasion. Each recipe is carefully selected to create a harmonious collection of flavors which includes main entrees, snacks, easy to make sauces, and fun cocktails.

Chef Dennis has a passion for teaching cooking classes; and he will teach you how to use Asian ingredients and spices to enhance flavors when preparing your meals. Simply put, food is his love language and it is interwoven into every aspect of his life. If he's not preparing food, he's tasting food, or thinking about what's next in food. If food is your passion, and you enjoy entertaining as much as Chef Dennis does, you already know that there is no greater joy than celebrating life around the dinner table.

This collection of recipes includes regional favorites such as Shrimp and Lobster Sauce, and BBQ Baked Pork Buns that are easy to prepare for casual dinners or intimate suppers. Also included are great party recipes, such as Sweet and Sour Ribs, Peking Pork Chops or Chinese Whiskey Sausage and Basil Fried Rice. In the chapter, "Dinner with Friends," you'll discover great foods to make your events memorable. If you're not into meat, try Blue Bamboo's Curried Rice Noodles or Cold Sesame Noodles. Look for easy appetizers such as Edamame Spread, or fun drinks such as an Almond Cookie Cocktail or a Dragon Cooler.

Cooking with the Cantonese-inspired recipes in "Let's Eat!" or "吃飯!" from Chef Dennis Chan will help create new memories that are sure to please not only the foodie in you, but also your family and friends!

Contents

Restaurant Legacy ••• p. 11

Blue Bamboo Edamame Spread — 11	Blue Bamboo Pork Dumplings — 13
Seared Sesame Chicken — 11	Soy Dipping Sauce — 13
Cucumber Smash Cocktail — 12	Almond Cookie Cocktail — 14
Duck Wonton Crisps — 12	Dragon Cooler — 14

Family Time ••• p. 15

Sweet and Sour Ribs — 15	Lotus Seed Bao — 19
Pork Shao Mai Dumplings — 16	Curry Beef Buns — 20
Longevity Pork Noodles — 17	Simple Qing Chao Ginger Garlic Bok Choy — 20
Congee Rice Porridge — 18	
Green Scallion Sauce — 18	

Dinner with Friends ••• p. 21

Hong Kong Style Portuguese Egg Tarts with Corn Crust — 21	Easy Sweet Chile Mac with Chicken Salad — 24
Honey-Garlic Basil Chicken Wings — 22	Chicken Toasts — 24
Canton Caipirinha — 22	Cold Sesame Noodles — 25
Blue Bamboo Curried Rice Noodles — 23	Cucumber Relish — 25

VIP Luncheon ••• p. 26

Classic Cantonese Shrimp Lo Mein — 26	Pineapple Topping for Baked Bun Dough — 29
Blue Bamboo Jade Cocktail — 26	Cocktail Bun Coconut Filling for Baked Bun Dough — 29
Four Pandas Fortune Cookies — 27	Hoisin Chicken Lettuce Wraps — 30
Baked Bun Dough — 28	

Wok Down Memory Lane ••• p. 31

Peking Pork Chops — 31	Lop Cheung Chinese Whiskey Sausage with Basil Fried Rice — 34
Chinese Hao You Gai Lan with Beef — 32	Cantonese Egg Rolls — 35
Caramel Pineapple Foster — 32	Pineapple Sweet and Sour Dipping Sauce — 36
Shrimp with Lobster Sauce — 33	Ginger Blue Cocktail — 36

Restaurant Legacy

Blue Bamboo Edamame Spread

Serves 8

1 lb edamame, shelled and peeled
½ c olive oil
1 tbsp garlic, minced
1 small onion, chopped
1 tbsp chopped fresh rosemary
Salt, to taste

In a medium pot, boil beans, garlic, and onion until tender (approx. 15 minutes). Strain items and reserve liquid. Place all the solid ingredients in a food processor. Puree, and season. Add reserved liquid if mixture is too thick. Can be served immediately, or refrigerate to serve cold. Spread on toast, crackers, or tortilla.

Seared Sesame Chicken

Serves 4

2 lbs chicken breast cutlets, pounded thin
Flour for dusting
2 tbsp neutral oil
1 tbsp peeled garlic, chopped
1 tsp ginger, minced
1 tbsp scallions, chopped
½ c honey
½ c soy sauce
½ c rice wine vinegar
½ c scallion tops, cut into 1 inch pieces

Salt and pepper to taste
Sesame seeds for garnish
Steamed broccoli for garnish

Dust cutlets in flour. Use a sauté pan and sear dusted cutlets over medium heat in oil. Flip over. Add ginger, garlic, scallion, honey, soy sauce, and vinegar. Bring to a boil, and simmer until chicken is done. Sprinkle with sesame seeds and scallion tops for garnish. Serve with steamed rice and broccoli.

Cucumber Smash Cocktail

Makes 1 Cocktail

1 – 1 inch pc cucumber
½ lime, muddled
1 oz simple syrup
2 oz vodka or sake
Chilled martini glass, lime

In a mixing glass or cocktail shaker, muddle cucumber and lime with sugar or simple syrup until flavors meld.
Add vodka or sake and ice. Stir.
Strain into chilled martini glass.

Duck Wonton Crisps

Serves 4

½ tsp ginger
½ tsp garlic
½ tsp scallion
3 tbsp roast duck, pulled and chopped
2 c veggies (carrots, onions, cabbage), shredded
2 tbsp hoisin sauce
2 tbsp sweet chili sauce
1 tbsp dry white wine
½ tbsp sesame oil
1 tbsp soy sauce
Salt and Pepper to taste
12 Fried wontons

Finishing sauces (Wasabi aioli, Sriracha mayonnaise, Red chili oil, Thai basil oil)

In a sauté pan, sauté ginger, garlic, and scallion until fragrant. Add veggies and duck. Sauté until veggies are tender.

Add seasonings. Cook until warmed through. Alternate wontons and duck and veggie mixture on your choice of plates. Finish dish with drizzled sauces.

Blue Bamboo Pork Dumplings

Serves 4

8 oz ground pork

6 oz Napa cabbage leaves, finely chopped

2 tsp ginger, finely chopped

1 tbsp Shaoxing rice wine or dry sherry

1 ½ tbsp soy sauce

1 tsp salt

½ tsp black pepper, freshly ground

3 tbsp green onions, finely chopped

2 tsp sesame oil

1 tsp sugar

2 tbsp cold chicken stock

1 pkg dumpling wrappers

Egg, beaten, for sealing

Combine filling ingredients until well mixed. Place rounded tablespoon in middle of wrapper. Fold and seal with egg. Bring a large pot of water to a boil. Drop half of the dumplings into the water and stir once so they don't stick together.

When the water boils again, add 1 cup of cold water to the pot. When it boils a second time, add 2 cups of cold water. The third time the water boils, the dumplings are cooked. Remove dumplings with a slotted spoon and repeat with the remaining dumplings.

Serve immediately with small bowls of dipping sauce.

Soy Dipping Sauce

Serves 4

½ tsp sugar

3 tbsp soy sauce

1 tbsp vinegar

Pepper to taste

Bring ingredients to a boil. Our favorite colorful garnish for this sauce is toasted sesame and green onion rings.

Almond Cookie Cocktail

Makes 1 Cocktail

½ oz almond liqueur
½ oz white creme de cacao
2 oz cream
Ice
Cherry for garnish
Stemmed cocktail glass

Place ice in shaker. Add almond liqueur, crème de cacao, and cream into shaker with ice. Shake until mixed well and chilled. Strain into glass and garnish with cherry.

Dragon Cooler

Makes 1 Cocktail

1 oz orange juice
2 oz pineapple juice
½ oz grenadine
1 oz white rum
Lemon-lime soda to fill glass
Crushed ice - enough to fill wine glass
Orange wheel and cherry for garnish
Wine glass

Place ice in blender. Add orange juice, pineapple juice, rum, and grenadine to blender and blend until smooth. Pour into wine glass and garnish with orange wheel and cherry.

Family Time

Sweet and Sour Ribs

Serves 4

- ½ c cucumbers, pickled and sliced
- ½ c tomatoes, quartered
- ½ c bell peppers, sliced
- ½ c onions, sliced
- ½ c pineapple chunks
- 1 ½ lb spare ribs, cut into 1" segments
- Flour, as needed
- 2 eggs, beaten into an egg-wash
- Neutral oil for frying

- ¼ c ketchup
- 1 c water
- 1 c vinegar
- 1 c sugar

Coat ribs in flour, egg-wash, and flour a second time. Fry in neutral oil in a deep pot or pan at 350 degrees until done. Place remaining ingredients into a wok or saucepan and bring to a boil. Add ribs to sauce, and cook for 1 minute, and toss to coat. Serve family style on a large platter with steamed rice.

Dennis Chan

Pork Shao Mai Dumplings "Roast and Sell" Dumplings

Serves 4

1 lb boneless pork shoulder, ground
2 oz pork fat, diced
¼ tsp ground white pepper
½ tsp kosher salt
2 tsp cornstarch
2 tsp Shaoxing rice cooking wine or dry sherry
1 tsp toasted sesame oil
1 tsp neutral oil
½ tsp peeled ginger, fresh and finely grated
½ tsp sugar
1 pkg wonton wrappers, extra-thin or regular
1 c short grain rice, soaked and steamed

Add pork and pork fat to the food processor and pulse until finely chopped.

Add white pepper, salt, cornstarch, Shaoxing wine, sesame oil, olive oil, ginger, and sugar to the pork. Mix well until thoroughly combined. Cover bowl, and set filling aside in the refrigerator for at least 30 minutes or overnight to allow flavors to meld.

Hold wonton wrapper in the palm of your hand. Place 1 tablespoon of filling in the middle of the wrapper. Gently squeeze sides to form an open-faced dumpling. Add 1 teaspoon of steamed sticky rice on top of filling and place in steamer basket, lined with parchment that has holes to allow steam to flow through. Repeat with remaining ingredients.

Arrange in the steamer tray, leaving room around each one and steaming in batches if necessary. Steam fresh shao mai until cooked through, about 7 minutes.

Place steamer basket, on a large platter and serve.

Longevity Pork Noodles

Serves 4

- 8 oz pork, minced
- 1 tbsp dark soy sauce
- 1 tsp salt
- 8 fl oz neutral oil
- 3 tbsp garlic, finely chopped
- 2 tbsp ginger root, peeled, and finely chopped
- 5 tbsp scallions, finely chopped
- 2 tbsp sesame paste or peanut butter
- 2 tbsp dark soy sauce
- 2-4 tbsp chili oil
- 2 tsp salt
- 8 fl oz chicken stock
- 12 oz Chinese thin egg noodles, fresh or dry Chinese thin egg noodles
- 1 tbsp Sichuan peppercorns (roasted and ground)

In a small bowl, combine the pork, soy sauce, and salt and mix well.

Heat a wok or deep frying pan until hot. Add the oil and deep-fry the pork. Break pork up into smaller pieces with the spatula. Cook for 3-4 minutes until the pork is crispy and dry. Remove the cooked mixture with a slotted spoon and drain in a separate bowl.

Set aside majority of used oil except for 2 tablespoons left in the wok. Reheat the wok and add the garlic, ginger, and onions and stir fry for 30 seconds. Then, add the sesame paste or peanut butter, soy sauce, chili oil, salt, and chicken stock and simmer for 4 minutes.

In a large pot, cook the noodles and boil in water for 2 minutes if the noodles are fresh. If store bought or dry, cook for 5 minutes. Drain the noodles well and divide the noodles into individual serving bowls.

Ladle on the sauce, garnish with the fried pork and Sichuan peppercorns and serve at once.

Congee Rice Porridge

Serves 4

- 3 ½ to 4-lb chicken, cut into serving pieces
- 10 c water
- 3 tbsp sherry, medium-dry
- 3 ginger, freshly sliced, ¼ inch-thick, and smashed well
- 3 scallions, halved crosswise and smashed
- ½ tsp salt and white pepper to taste
- 1 c rice, long-grain

Green Scallion Sauce

Serves 4

- 1 bch scallions, (green part only)
- ¼ c spinach, blanched
- Neutral Oil
- Salt and Pepper to taste

Place in all items in blender. Puree until smooth. Serve alongside dumplings and soy sauce. Sauce can be made 2 hours ahead, and stored until ready for service.

Bring chicken and water to a boil in a 5-quart or larger pot, skimming froth. Add sherry, ginger, scallions, salt and simmer uncovered for 20 minutes. Remove chicken meat and set aside. Return skin and bones to pot and simmer for 2 hours. Add additional liquid if stock evaporates too quickly. Cool chicken meat and shred. Set aside in refrigerator to use as garnish.

Strain stock with a strainer or colander and discard solids. Return 2 quarts of stock to the large pot, bring to a boil and add rice. Reduce heat to a low stove top setting, and simmer covered for 1 ½ hours. Check on the stock and stir frequently during last ½ hour of cooking. If the porridge becomes too thick, thin with additional stock.

Alternative Preparation:

Place ingredients in a pressure cooker such as an Instant pot and pressure cook for 30 minutes, plus, natural release.
Season congee with salt and white pepper. Serve topped with chicken and green onion, and your favorite toppings in your favorite bowls.

Lotus Seed Bao

Serves 4, 16 buns total

Steamed Buns:

1 c warm water (105-115°F)

½ tsp active dry yeast

4 tbsp sugar, plus a pinch

2 tbsp nonfat dried milk

¼ c pork fat, lard, or duck fat

3 ½ c bread flour

1 ½ tsp kosher salt

1 ½ tsp baking powder

Pinch of baking soda

Neutral oil for greasing and brushing

Lotus seed paste. Available at your local Asian market.

In a large bowl, mix dried yeast with warm water and milk powder. Add a tablespoon of rendered pork fat and mix well.

In a mixer, combine bread flour, salt, and sugar.

Slowly pour in the water, yeast and fat mixture. Use a dough hook and knead the mixture for 13-15 minutes. It will be wet and sticky. Transfer the dough to a lightly oiled bowl, cover with a damp towel and let rise for two hours.

Once the dough has doubled in size, knock it back down and on a clean counter, roll dough into a long log shape. If it is too sticky, add little flour.

Cut it into 16 even sized pieces and let rise for another thirty minutes on a sheet pan lined with baking paper.

Cut out 16 squares of baking paper, each about four inches square.

Roll each ball of dough into an oval shape, about the size of your hand, flatten, fill with lotus seed paste, pinch edges to close, and place onto the square of baking paper. Let rise for thirty minutes.

Set a bamboo or metal steamer over a pan of boiling water and steam the buns for about eight to ten minutes until they are pillow-y and puffy. Serve immediately.

Curry Beef Buns

Serves 4

- 6 oz ground beef
- ⅓ c chopped onion
- 1 tbsp cooking oil
- 1 tbsp dry sherry
- 1 tbsp soy sauce
- 1 tbsp curry powder
- 2 tsp sweet chile sauce
- 2 tsp corn starch
- Neutral oil

Pan fry beef and onion in neutral oil until cooked thoroughly. Add sauce ingredients and bring to a boil. Remove from heat and transfer to dish or bowl. Let cool in refrigerator. Pre-heat oven to 350°. *Stuff buns and bake until golden and done for 16-18 minutes.

* Use the recipe on page 28 for Baked Bun Dough.

Simple Qing Chao Ginger-Garlic Bok Choy

Serves 4

- 1 tsp ginger
- 1 tsp garlic
- 2 tbsp neutral oil
- 1 pound bok choy, or other leafy green vegetable, washed and air-dried
- salt to taste
- pepper to taste
- 1 tbsp cornstarch slurry
    (1:1 corn starch and water)

Heat wok. Add oil to heated pan, and ginger and garlic. Add bok choy and toss to coat. Stir until wilted. Season with salt and pepper. Toss with slurry and serve.

LET'S EAT!

Dinner with Friends

Hong Kong Style Portuguese Egg Tarts with Corn Crust
Serves 4 / Yields 8 tarts

7 tbsp butter, at room temperature
¾ c sugar
1 egg
⅔ c flour
4 tbsp corn meal, fine
⅓ c corn powder, freeze-dried
½ tsp baking powder
⅛ tsp baking soda
½ tsp kosher salt

4 egg yolks
⅓ c of sugar
⅓ c of heavy cream
⅓ c of milk
3 drops of vanilla extract

In a mixing bowl, or you can whisk by hand, cream butter and sugar together. Add the egg and beat for 7-8 minutes.
In a separate bowl, add all of the remaining ingredients and stir until just mixed.
Combine dry ingredients into butter, egg, and sugar mixture.
Scoop even portions of dough, and form them in tart shells. Freeze until solid.

As an alternative short-cut, you can find tart shells in your grocer freezer isle.
Combine filling ingredients and strain into the frozen tart shells.

Preheat the oven to 350 degrees. Bake for 18 minutes, or until tops are slightly browned with spots, and the filling slightly jiggles. Serve on your favorite platter.

Cool before consuming.

Dennis Chan

Honey-Garlic Basil Chicken Wings
Serves 4

8 lg chicken wings, whole.
1 tbsp fish sauce
1 tbsp garlic, chopped
2 tbsp sugar
1 ½ c water

Flour, to coat
3 tbsp honey
3 tbsp soy sauce
1 tsp ginger, minced
1 tbsp corn starch, mixed with 2 tbsp water
3 sprigs of basil
3 tbsp fried shallots

Marinate chicken wings in garlic, sugar, and water overnight in refrigerator.

Dredge wings in flour and fry in 350 degrees oil until done. Remove from oil and drain.

In a sauté pan over medium heat, bring soy, honey, ginger, and used marinade to a boil. Add half of shallots and corn starch and water to thicken sauce. Toss wings in sauce and garnish with fresh basil and remaining fried shallots. Serve on a platter or decorative bowl.

Canton Caipirinha (Brazil's official cocktail, by way of Canton…)
Makes 1 Cocktail

½ lime muddled
1½ oz cachaca
½ oz canton ginger liqueur
½ oz simple syrup or 1 tbsp sugar
Wedge of lime for garnish

In a cocktail shaker, muddle lime and simple syrup or sugar. Add ice, cachaça, plus ginger liqueur. Stir. Strain into rocks glass, filled with ice. Garnish with a wedge of lime.

Blue Bamboo Curried Rice Noodles

Serves 4

1 lb dried rice noodles, re-hydrated
1 tbsp neutral oil for stir-frying.
½ tsp fresh ginger, minced
½ tsp garlic, minced
1 tbsp scallions, chopped
1 c onions, sliced
½ c carrots, shredded
1 c green vegetables of choice.
1 c chicken broth
¼ c coconut cream or coconut milk
1 tbsp fish sauce
2 tsp sugar
1 tbsp curry powder
Fresh herbs for garnish (basil, cilantro, micro herbs)

Soak rice noodles in warm water for 20 minutes. Drain. Using a wok or sauté pan, heat oil and add ginger and garlic and scallion. Add curry powder, onion, carrots, and veggies. Sauté until vegies are tender. Add coconut milk and chicken broth. Bring to a boil. Add sugar and fish sauce.

After mixture is bubbling, add noodles. When noodles have softened, divide into bowls or serve on a platter, family style. Garnish with fresh herbs.

Easy Sweet Chile Mac with Chicken Salad

Serves 4

1 - 1 lb package macaroni, cooked to manufacturer's directions
1 c sweet chili sauce
½ c soy sauce
1 c total shredded carrots, cabbage, red onions, and peppers
1 c grilled chicken, cut into cubes
Fresh herbs

In a large mixing bowl, combine ingredients. Set aside in refrigerator for flavors to meld. Serve individually, in bowls, martini glasses, or on a platter.

Chicken Toasts

Serves 4

½ lb chicken breast
1 tbsp sherry
1 tbsp soy sauce
2 tbsp corn starch
2 egg whites
4 slices white bread
½ c sesame seeds
Neutral oil for deep frying

In a food processor bowl, add chicken, sherry, soy sauce, and corn starch. Process until combined well. Whisk egg whites until stiff peaks. Fold into chicken mixture.

Cut each bread slice into 4 squares or triangles. Spread chicken paste on each piece of bread. Coat with sesame seeds.

Heat oil until 375°F. Fry until golden. Remove from oil and place on a clean paper towel to absorb some oil. Serve on your favorite platter with cucumber relish and sweet chili dipping sauce.

Cold Sesame Noodles
Serves 6

1 ½ lb egg noodles, fresh or frozen from your local Asian market
2 tbsp sesame oil
4 tbsp soy sauce
2 tbsp rice wine vinegar
2 tbsp Tahini or sesame paste
2 tbsp peanut butter
1 tbsp sugar
1 tbsp ginger, grated
1 tbsp garlic, minced
1 tbsp chili paste (to taste)
Sliced raw cucumber and peanuts and sesame seeds, for garnish

Cook noodles until tender, and center is done, about 5 minutes.

Drain and cool in ice water to stop cooking. Drain. Combine sesame oil, soy sauce, vinegar, sesame paste, peanut butter, sugar, ginger, garlic, and chile paste in a medium bowl. Whisk to combine. Add noodles to sauce and toss. Serve on a platter, garnished with peanuts, sesame seeds, and sliced cucumber.

Cucumber Relish
Serves 4

1 English cucumber, sliced
2 shallots, sliced
2 tbsp cilantro, chopped
½ c rice vinegar
3 tsp sugar
¼ tsp salt
Chopped peanuts for garnish

Combine all ingredients. Let marinate in refrigerator for 10 minutes to allow flavors to meld. Serve as a side to compliment any fried foods.

Dennis Chan ••• 25

VIP Luncheon

Classic Cantonese Shrimp Lo Mein

Serves 2

- 8 oz Chinese egg noodles, fresh
- 2 tbsp neutral oil
- 6 oz shrimp, peeled and de-veined
- 3 cloves garlic, smashed and minced
- 1 c carrots, sliced thin
- 2 celery stalks, sliced thin
- ⅓ c green peppers, sliced thin
- ¼ c bamboo shoots, julienned
- 3 green onions, sliced thin
- 3 tbsp oyster-flavored sauce
- 1 tbsp soy sauce
- 1 ½ tsp sesame oil

In a large pot of boiling water, cook noodles according to package instructions; drain, rinse with cold water and drain.

Place a stir-fry pan over high heat until hot. Add oil, swirling to coat sides. Add garlic and cook, stirring, until fragrant, about 5 seconds. Add carrots, celery, green peppers, bamboo shoots, and green onions. Stir-fry until vegetables wilt slightly, 2-3 minutes.

Add noodles, oyster-flavored sauce, soy sauce, and sesame oil. Toss to mix noodles with vegetables and cook until all vegetables are tender, about 2 minutes. Serve immediately.

Blue Bamboo Jade Cocktail

Makes 1 Cocktail

- 1 oz vodka
- ½ oz blue curacao
- ½ oz triple sec
- Splash orange juice
- Orange slice, for garnish

Chilled martini glass or champagne flute

In a cocktail shaker filled with ice, pour in ingredients. Shake. Strain into chilled martini glass. Garnish with orange slice or twist.

Four Pandas Fortune Cookies

Makes 30 fortune cookies

3 egg whites
¾ c sugar
½ c butter, melted
¼ tsp lemon extract
1 c all-purpose flour
2 tbsp water
¼ teaspoon vanilla extract
Pinch of salt
2 ½ x ½ in. fortune strips, prepared.

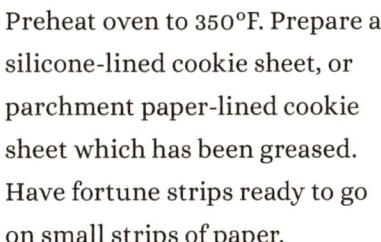

Preheat oven to 350°F. Prepare a silicone-lined cookie sheet, or parchment paper-lined cookie sheet which has been greased. Have fortune strips ready to go on small strips of paper.

In a stand mixer, whip egg whites and sugar on high speed until frothy.

Reduce speed to low, and stir in melted butter, vanilla, lemon extract, water and flour. Working in batches of three, use a spoon to drop a teaspoon of the batter onto the lined cookie sheet.

Shape batter into 3 inch circles with room between for spreading. Bake for 5 to 7 minutes in oven until the edges are a light golden color.

Quickly remove the cookies with a spatula one at a time, and place a fortune strip in the center. Fold the ends of the half together into a U shape. Hold until cool enough to set.

Repeat with remaining batter.

Baked Bun Dough

Makes 12 buns

3 ¾ c flour

⅓ c sugar

¼ oz active dry yeast

1 tsp salt

⅓ c butter, softened

½ c milk, warmed

½ c water, warmed

1 egg

In a bowl, combine sugar, warm milk, and yeast.

In a mixer bowl, add warm tap water to the butter and warm to approximately 100°. Combine. Add egg and salt.

Add flour until a soft dough is formed in mixer. Using dough hook, knead for 5 minutes. Place dough in a large glass or metal bowl and cover with a clean towel. Let rise until doubled in size in approximately 1 hour. Punch down the dough and let rise again until it's doubled in another 1 hour.

Divide dough into 12 equal pieces, fill with filling and shape into round buns. Place on baking sheets, cover with a slightly damp towel, and let rise until doubled (about 45 minutes).

Pineapple Topping for Baked Buns
Makes 12 bun toppings

¼ c sugar
⅛ c butter
1 egg yolk
½ tsp baking soda
1 tbsp milk
½ c flour
1 tsp baking powder

Note: These baked buns are a Hong Kong bakery staple. Although they are named pineapple buns, there is no pineapple in the recipe. The buns get their name from the topping which looks like a pineapple's outer skin when it is baked.

Beat butter and sugar until creamy and fluffy. Add egg yolk, soda, and milk. Mix well. Sift flour and baking powder into the butter mixture. Mix by hand until smooth and not sticky. Roll out your chilled bun topping to a ¼ inch. Wrap and chill for 1 hour, until solid. Cut out circles to fit over buns. Brush the buns with water, and layer on topping. Lightly score in a crisscross pattern, and brush buns with reserved egg. Bake at 375° for 13 minutes, until slightly golden. Cool slightly and serve.

Cocktail Bun Coconut Filling for Baked Buns
Coconut Filling for 12 buns

1 c coconut flakes
1 tbsp sugar
2 tbsp butter, melted
1 egg yolk

In a food processor, add coconut and sugar and process until very fine. Transfer to a bowl.

Add in butter and egg yolk until paste-like consistency. Place filling into a pastry bag with a small tip. Form dough into pocket and pipe filling into bun. Seal bun and garnish top of bun with additional filling. Brush with egg wash and bake at 350° for 13 minutes, until slightly golden. Cool slightly and serve.

Hoisin Chicken Lettuce Wraps

Serves 4

1 carrot, julienned
1 zucchini, julienned
1 red onion, sliced
1 lettuce head, leaves separated, for wrapping
1 tbsp Sweet Chile Sauce
1 tbsp Hoisin Sauce
1 tsp orange zest, optional
1 tsp soy sauce
½ tsp sriracha
1 tsp fresh, minced ginger
½ tsp fresh garlic
Neutral oil for stir frying
Crushed peanuts, for garnish

Heat oil in wok or sauté pan.
Add garlic and ginger, and vegetables.
Add sauces.
Cook until ingredients are softened.
Serve in lettuce leaves, or alongside lettuce leaves. Garnish with peanuts.

Wok Down Memory Lane

Peking Pork Chops

Serves 4

- 1 ½ lb pork chops, cut into 2 inch pieces
- 1 ½ c flour for coating
- 1 ½ tbsp tomato ketchup
- ½ tbsp plum sauce
- ½ tbsp chili sauce
- ¼ tsp sweet bean sauce, or Hoisin sauce
- 1 tbsp Worcestershire sauce
- 1 ½ tbsp black vinegar
- 1 ½ tbsp sugar
- Small pinch of Chinese five spice powder
- 2 tbsp water
- ½ yellow onion, sliced
- Oil, for frying

Flour pork chops and fry in shallow oil in sauté pan until done. Set aside.

In a sauté pan, bring remaining ingredients to a boil. Toss in pork chops to coat and serve on your favorite platter.

Dennis Chan

Chinese Hao You Gai Lan (Chinese Broccoli) with Beef

Serves 4

½ lb beef, cut into strips
2 c gailan, or Chinese broccoli, cut into 2" pieces, blanched
1 tbsp ginger
1 tbsp garlic
1 tbsp scallion
1 tbsp neutral oil
3 tbsp oyster Sauce
½ c chicken broth
1 tbsp corn starch, mixed with 2 tbsp water

Pre-heat wok to medium-high heat. Add oil. Swirl to coat pan. Sauté ginger, garlic, and scallion until fragrant. Add beef, vegetables and broth. Bring to a boil. Toss until desired doneness. Add oyster sauce and toss to coat. Drizzle in corn starch and water as needed to tighten up sauce. Serve over steamed rice in bowls.

Caramel Pineapple Foster

Serves 4

1 c brown sugar
½ c half-and-half
3 tbsp butter, cubed
Pinch salt
Sliced Pineapple, one whole, cut into 1 inch pieces
Ice cream, for plating

Mix the brown sugar, half-and-half, butter and salt in a saucepan over medium-low heat. Cook for 2 – 5 minutes, until caramelized. Add pineapples. Cook until desired tenderness, approximately 5 minutes. Serve with your favorite ice cream.

Shrimp with Lobster Sauce

Serves 4

- 1 ½ tsp cornstarch
- 2 tsp cooking sherry
- 1 lb medium shrimp - peeled and de-veined
- 4 tbsp vegetable oil
- 2 cloves garlic, minced
- ¼ lb ground pork
- 1 c chicken stock
- 2 tbsp soy sauce
- ¼ tsp sugar
- ½ tsp salt
- 1 ½ tbsp cornstarch
- ¼ c cold water
- 1 egg, beaten

In a medium bowl, dissolve 1 ½ teaspoons of cornstarch in the sherry. Add shrimp to the bowl, and toss to coat.

Heat oil in a wok or large skillet over medium-high heat. Add shrimp, and fry until pink, 3 to 5 minutes. Remove shrimp to a plate with a slotted spoon, leaving as much oil in the pan as possible. Add garlic to the hot oil with the ground pork. Toss on heat until pork is no longer pink.

Remove extra oil and add chicken stock, soy sauce, sugar and salt; stir into the wok with the pork. Bring to a boil, cover, reduce heat to medium, and simmer for 2 minutes. Mix together the remaining 1 ½ tablespoons of cornstarch and ¼ cup cold water. Pour into the pan with the pork, and also shrimp to the pan. Return to a simmer, and stir while drizzling in the beaten egg. Cook until curds form. Serve hot over rice.

Lop Cheung Chinese Whiskey Sausage and Basil Fried Rice

Serves 2

¼ cup onion, sliced

¼ cup carrots, shredded

2 cups long grain rice, cooked and cooled

2 links Lop Cheung Sausage

1 egg

2 tbsp canola oil, for frying

½ tsp salt

½ tsp pepper

2 tbsp soy sauce

Additional diced vegetables, herbs, and protein of choice.

Thai Basil, leaves only

Start with cold, cooked rice.

Heat a wok or sauté pan to medium heat. Add oil. Gently break an egg into the hot oil. Swirl it around to cook. Add Lop Cheung sausage and onions. Cook for about 2 minutes.

Add cold rice and stir, toasting all sides of each grain. Add carrots. Add salt, pepper, and soy sauce. Stir. Be careful, rice will want to stick to pan. Stir until heated through. Add Basil and toss.

Serve and garnish with sliced green onions, and fresh herbs.

Shrimp with Lobster Sauce

Serves 4

- 1 ½ tsp cornstarch
- 2 tsp cooking sherry
- 1 lb medium shrimp - peeled and de-veined
- 4 tbsp vegetable oil
- 2 cloves garlic, minced
- ¼ lb ground pork
- 1 c chicken stock
- 2 tbsp soy sauce
- ¼ tsp sugar
- ½ tsp salt
- 1 ½ tbsp cornstarch
- ¼ c cold water
- 1 egg, beaten

In a medium bowl, dissolve 1 ½ teaspoons of cornstarch in the sherry. Add shrimp to the bowl, and toss to coat.

Heat oil in a wok or large skillet over medium-high heat. Add shrimp, and fry until pink, 3 to 5 minutes. Remove shrimp to a plate with a slotted spoon, leaving as much oil in the pan as possible. Add garlic to the hot oil with the ground pork. Toss on heat until pork is no longer pink.

Remove extra oil and add chicken stock, soy sauce, sugar and salt; stir into the wok with the pork. Bring to a boil, cover, reduce heat to medium, and simmer for 2 minutes. Mix together the remaining 1 ½ tablespoons of cornstarch and ¼ cup cold water. Pour into the pan with the pork, and also shrimp to the pan. Return to a simmer, and stir while drizzling in the beaten egg. Cook until curds form. Serve hot over rice.

Lop Cheung Chinese Whiskey Sausage and Basil Fried Rice
Serves 2

¼ cup onion, sliced

¼ cup carrots, shredded

2 cups long grain rice, cooked and cooled

2 links Lop Cheung Sausage

1 egg

2 tbsp canola oil, for frying

½ tsp salt

½ tsp pepper

2 tbsp soy sauce

Additional diced vegetables, herbs, and protein of choice.

Thai Basil, leaves only

Start with cold, cooked rice.

Heat a wok or sauté pan to medium heat. Add oil. Gently break an egg into the hot oil. Swirl it around to cook. Add Lop Cheung sausage and onions. Cook for about 2 minutes.

Add cold rice and stir, toasting all sides of each grain. Add carrots. Add salt, pepper, and soy sauce. Stir. Be careful, rice will want to stick to pan. Stir until heated through. Add Basil and toss.

Serve and garnish with sliced green onions, and fresh herbs.

Cantonese Egg Rolls

Serves 4

¼ lb roast pork (optional)

¼ lb ground chicken, cooked (optional)

4 oz re-hydrated mung bean noodle available in the Asian aisle of local markets

1 c shredded cabbage, blanched

½ c shredded carrots

½ c shredded celery, blanched

¼ c sliced green onion

Salt and pepper, to taste

Sesame oil, to taste

Frozen egg roll skins

Egg, for sealing

Soak mung bean noodle in hot water until soft. (Approximately 10 minutes)

Drain and rinse under cold water.

Cut all vegetables to size, and blanch if desired. Squeeze all water out of ingredients after blanched and cooled to room temperature. Combine chicken and pork, bean noodle, cabbage, carrots, celery, green onion, salt, pepper, and sesame oil in a large mixing bowl. Roll filling in wrapper, as if you are making a tight burrito.

Fry at 350° oil until golden brown. Drain on a clean paper towel and serve on your favorite dinner platter.

Pineapple Sweet and Sour Dipping Sauce

Serves 4

½ c pineapple preserves
1 c applesauce
Salt and pepper
Honey, to taste
2 tbsp white vinegar

Heat small saucepan. Add ingredients and bring to boil. Cool and let stand for 1 hour. Add salt and pepper to taste.

Ginger Blue Cocktail

Makes 1 Cocktail

1 oz ginger liqueur
3 lime slices, muddled
Splash ginger ale
½ oz blue curacao
½ oz triple sec
Chilled martini glass

In a cocktail shaker, muddle lime slices. Add ice and remaining ingredients, stir, and strain into chilled martini glass. Garnish with a citrus ring.

Dennis Chan

Jacksonville's culinary star, Dennis Chan, creates memorable experiences through his food. He started working in his family's restaurants at a young age, and is the proud proprietor of Blue Bamboo Canton Bistro in Jacksonville, Florida.

Dennis Chan's training took place at the University of Florida, and the prestigious Culinary Institute of America, followed by an internship with Ming Tsai (PBS' Simply Ming). His customer service skills were meticulously polished while working for the Disney Company. Following his formal education, Chan landed in Winter Park, Florida as a manager for a growing restaurant company, where he forged his CIA training and customer service skills into becoming a well-rounded entrepreneur.

A great chef, cooking class teacher, college professor, businessman, community servant, father, and author, Dennis Chan now shares his passion for food in order to inspire others. He creates classic Cantonese comfort food with hints of French, Italian, Asian, and Southern accents, and his Blue Bamboo menu welcomes guests with excitement.

Over the years, Chan has cultivated devoted patrons because he regards the customer service experience equally as important as the quality ingredients he uses. His customers rave about his satisfying menu items and are delighted in Blue Bamboo Canton Bistro's relaxing vibe.

Chan says, "I honestly feel privileged to do what I love in the community I grew up in." He shares his family legacy through his restaurant, cooking classes, development of staff, and recipe books, all in the name of service to the community.

In 2018, Chan's Sunshine State Orange Crunch Cake won the General Mills Neighborhood to Nation Recipe Contest and in 2022 he was named SBA Florida Businessperson of the Year. A fitting reward for a well-loved son of Jacksonville.

www.ingramcontent.com/pod-product-compliance
Lightning Source LLC
Chambersburg PA
CBHW042306150426
43197CB00001B/33